PHOENIX FORMULA

Reinventing Yourself And Your Business

ONE STEP AT A TIME

JASON DROHN

Copyright © 2013 Jason Drohn
All rights reserved.

ISBN: 0989216802
ISBN-13: 9780989216807

Table of Contents

1 IT DIDN'T HAPPEN...   1

1.1 BEING PART OF THE PROBLEM	6
1.2 DIDN'T KNOW WHAT TO DO	10
1.3 TRAPPED IN INACTION	12
1.4 QUICKEST PATH TO CASH	14
1.5 FIND JOY IN A SMILE	15
1.6 BURN THE BOATS	17
1.7 NO WAY OUT	18

2 SELF ASSESSMENT   21

2.1 THINK	24
2.2 GET TO KNOW YOURSELF	27

3 GOALS AND PLANNING   31

3.1 SET GOALS BASED ON SELF ASSESSMENT	31
3.2 VISION	34
3.3 WHERE DO YOU WANT TO BE	36
3.4 REDEFINE SUCCESS	37
3.5 PLANNING	40

4 TAKING ACTION   45

4.1 PERSONAL MISSION STATEMENT	47
4.2 ACTION LISTS	50
4.3 SCHEDULE TO ACT	56
4.4 THE EPIC DOWNFALL?	58
4.5 TO DO LISTS	61
4.6 WHAT'S WORKING?	64
4.7 ONE PATH	70
4.8 DON'T GIVE UP	73
4.9 INSPIRATION	76

4.10 JOURNALING	78
4.11 STOP BUYING STUFF	79
4.12 EATING RIGHT	81
4.13 EXERCISE	83

5 SURROUNDINGS — 85

5.1 NO MORE NEGATIVE	86
5.2 FRIENDS	88
5.3 FAMILY	90
5.4 MINDSET	91
5.5 NEGATIVE ATTITUDE	96
5.6 BE AROUND PEOPLE THAT ARE BETTER THAN YOU	98
5.7 SHOP AT THE STORES YOU FEEL GOOD AT	100
5.8 GIVING	102

6 EDUCATION — 105

6.1 REINVEST	106
6.2 THINKING ROOM	107
6.3 MENTAL FUEL	108
6.4 PRACTICE YOUR CRAFT	109

7 CLOSING — 111

1

it didn't happen...

The year 2009 didn't happen in my mind. Frankly, I don't remember much of it. I remember instances where I was sitting on the front porch, staring at my neighbor's house, wondering how I was ever going to get out of the hole I had gotten myself in.

I remember waiting for my dogs to come in from outside, looking at the stars and asking myself how I was going to come up with the thousands of dollars that bill collectors were blowing up my phone for.

You see, my web design business collapsed. I had about 30 customers, some set up on recurring billing and others were not. In February 2009, all the news talked about was recession and layoffs and how the world was going to implode...

The small businesses that were my clients were going out of business left and right. They stopped paying their monthly bills. New business? All gone. No one had any money to spend. If they did, they weren't going to spend it on a website!

it didn't happen...

I do remember the day, keenly, that I logged into my bank account and there was no more money. I didn't have any invoices going out. I didn't have any checks to put in the bank. It was just all gone.

I had failed.

Two straight days were spent staring out my window...

All I could help thinking was that the world had come to an end. It had to have, right? EVERYTHING in my life stopped.

I had no where to go...

I had no money to get anywhere... I had no clients who had money that I could go sell anything to...

What followed was about 6 months of sheer hell.

I was afraid of going outside for fear of a bill collector showing up at my door.

Everywhere I looked, I felt that people knew I was a failure... That my business crumbled beneath my feet and I didn't have money to do anything!

There was one time my girlfriend went to the store to find something for dinner. She came back and said her debit card was declined for $1.98. She found a box of pasta and some sauce for $.99 each and had to come back home to get the last $2.00 we had.

I actually got 52 calls in one day from bill collectors… I had to turn my cell phone off… And then Verizon shut off my service for lack of payment.

That was my 2009.

That, my friends, is not why you're reading this book though… To hear about my shitty existence 'way' back then. Nor is that why I'm writing for you today.

It's the beginning of 2011 right now. Since then, I've had the most extraordinary, mind- numbingly amazing life that anyone can possibly imagine.

Now, I'm not talking about rags to riches, fancy cars and big houses. I'm talking about success.

More notably, how small successes can lead to bigger successes and the realization of dreams and goals.

The tail of 2009 and all of 2010 was dedicated to rebuilding and reinventing.

I challenged EVERYTHING I knew and learned a lot of new stuff. I broke out of my comfort zone. I lived every day as if it was my last. I worked my ass off, sometimes 20 hours a day. I learned A LOT and tested a lot.

That reinvention led to me stepping up as an Internet marketing consultant and doing SEO and stuff for high-end clients.

I also got heavy into affiliate marketing, where I helped companies sell their products online for a commission through simple websites or email marketing.

Both disciplines used what I already knew from my failed web design business, but in a way that wasn't directly tied to the familiar equation of trading time for money.

That was a big step in the right direction.

Now, this isn't a book about Internet marketing or starting a business or a blog, but I publish plenty of that kind of information on Money Sites (http://moneysites.com).

You'll get an inside look at what works, why it works, and how to set up similar systems for yourself.

For now though, let's stay the course.

As you know 2009, everything fell apart. Between 2009 and 2011, here's some of the stuff I've been privileged to:

- Made friends with some of the top Internet marketers and 'thinkers' in the world.
- Have gotten closer to my girlfriend of 5 years than I've ever been before (it's amazing what sudden poverty can do to a relationship…)
- Am able to have a client list of people most consultants would die for… All paying lots every month to work with me.
- Attended some of the most amazing conferences and events in the country.

- Launched my first successful digital product.
- Been listed with some of the top affiliates in the world on product launches.
- Make over $6,000 a month in affiliate income without spending any money for traffic
- Have over 110 websites, 25 or so of which make me money daily.

I'm not telling you this to point out all the things I have (or have started) that you don't. I'm not trying to do that at all.

I just want you to be aware that in 2009, I didn't have anything. No friends. No money. No clients. Few website properties (and the ones I did have made very little money)…

I shut down.

I remember thinking that the **only thing that would save me is time**. All I had to do was get through this minute.

This hour. This day. Because… One day, I would make it. I'd have everything I wanted. I'd be successful. I'd have my company and I would be able to choose who I wanted to work with and who I didn't. And my girlfriend (wife) would be able to afford a new purse or good food…

She wouldn't have to worry about paying her student loans or wonder what we were going to have for dinner or that we didn't have enough money for her to go out to lunch with her friends…

it didn't happen...

In this book, I want to share with you my exact blueprint, or formula, for getting to where I am so that you can model it and use it to break through any and all barriers that come your way...

... So you can start taking action and making incredible money.

... So you can finally get out of debt.

... So you can build an incredible relationship with your partner or your significant other.

... So you can BREAK OUT of the ho-hum daily lifestyle that you're caught up in and finally SUCCEED!

This guide is going to teach you how to take action and achieve ANYTHING. Bottom line. Are you ready to get started?

1.1 BEING PART OF THE PROBLEM

Standing in the basement of my grandma's house, looking confused and really just wanting to go play Mega Man on my first generation Nintendo my parents just bought me, I stood listening to my dad explain how he wanted me to help him.

My dad. He worked his tail off to help support my 3 brothers, my mom and I. His main job was at a chemical company that manufactured a lot of the solvents and liquids that you can buy at a store. Things like WD40 or windshield wiper fluid.

He was a plant manager, so he knew a thing or two about leadership and positive thinking. That job required about 60 hours a week worth of time and he had a little part time gig that he worked one night a week. On weekends, he picked up side projects that would bring in a little extra money.

Guess who was his little helper buddy? Yep. Me.

I was the oldest of the bunch, so of course I got roped into a lot of weird drywall projects or painting or powerwashing…

Me being only 7, kind of despised it because my friends were outside playing while I was working around the house…

Needless to say, I learned a lot. I had to learn what all the tools were named so I could get them when he asked. I learned all about home repair… So much so that now, around my own house, I will try to fix something and just kinda 'know what to do' without really 'knowing how to do it.'

It's a weird feeling for sure. Last year, we remodeled our bathroom and at the start of the project, I had no idea what to do. I knew we would need paint and spackling and sandpaper. I didn't know exactly what came next though… But as I was working, it just 'felt' right to me.

The bathroom - fantastic. Nothing revolutionary but it was a drastic facelift, which is what we were looking for.

Anyway, working with my dad…
The first time I helped him with a project, he knelt down beside me and taught me about anticipation. "Chip (my

it didn't happen...

nickname), I want you to watch what I'm doing, and try to figure out what I'm going to need next. Once you figure it out, go get it and wait until I'm ready."

At first, I was like "Whatever! I'm just going to hang out on my bucket and think about my Nintendo."

After a bit of hanging out, wondering what I was doing in my grandma's basement when she had cookies upstairs in the cupboard, my dad knelt down beside me to offer lesson #2.

"Chip, I want to explain something to you that's even more important than you anticipating what I'm going to need next. It's about problems and solutions."

"See, as you know, I work with guys all day long who are on the path to no where quick. Some of them are convicted felons. Some are high school drop outs. Some bad mouth their girlfriends and wives and mistreat their kids…"

"There are two ways to go about life. You can either be part of the problem or part of the solution. Being part of the problem will land in you jail or unemployed or worse. Being the solution means you have to take action and actively help other people succeed. Only then will you succeed yourself."

"Take this drywall for instance. You're too young to be sanding and applying spackle, but you can get me tools. By getting me tools, you're part of the solution because we'll be able to finish faster and get out of here quicker. I don't like working any more than you do but I do it so we can afford our lifestyle. All I need is for you to be part of the solution…"

So, I started to watch him work... He's spackling the wall. It's drying. What's the next step after spackling??? Sanding. That's right.

Ok, what's he going to need to do to sand? Sandpaper!

And he's using that weird block looking thing to make sure it's straight...

I go over and pick up the sander...

My dad, watching the whole thing out of the corner of his eye, turned around and started smiling! "That's it Chip. You anticipated that I'd be sanding next and that's going to save me lots of time and we're going to be able to get out of here sooner so you can go play your video games!"

That made me smile!

It was times like those that I thought about when he passed away. My dad and I weren't phenomenally close, but he taught me some incredibly important lessons early on that have helped a lot in my life.

It's weird how something so small as 'being part of the solution' can impact you life in such an incredible way...

In 2009, looking out the window as my business crumbled, I remembered this little story... About me sitting on the bucket so ready to go play video games or raid my grandma's cookie jar.

it didn't happen...

...And about my dad talking about being part of the solution and anticipated action.

1.2 DIDN'T KNOW WHAT TO DO

Sitting there, I had no idea what to do. Truly, I had no ideas. I was usually pretty good at getting myself out of these binds but I didn't have anything...

I was stumped.

I couldn't continue doing websites for small businesses because SO MANY small businesses were going under (hence, my predicament).

I had to do something though.

That's the only way to get anywhere in life! **Action...**

I started watching some of the product launches online and these guys generating incredible money very, very quickly. I figured I needed to start a few websites and sell them or make money with affiliate products.

After all, I already knew how to build websites. That's what I used to do for local businesses! But I had never thought to build a website that solved other people's problems and monetize it with affiliate products.

So, I sought out some education.

Not college or anything like that. I already had 2 college degrees and they weren't helping me that much...

So, I found a video course online that taught about putting these little niche websites together and how to sell affiliate products or your own ebooks.

That course is called Niche Profit Classroom (http://moneysites.com/npc/).

The premise was pretty simple. Niche Profit Classroom teaches building niche websites that generate little bits of money every month. $500. $1000.

So, after I started with the $1 trial (the biggest reason for choosing the course since I didn't have much money), I started registering domain names and throwing them on the hosting account that I had through my broken company.

I started 30 or 40 websites. I'd do lead capture pages and a few articles and move on to the next.

The topics were all over the place... Powerpoint presentations. Creating business slogans. Setting up social media accounts. I just needed one to make some cash.

You know what happened? Nothing. Nada.

None of the websites were getting any traffic!

And because I was all over the place and creating all these new web properties, I didn't have any time to write articles. I didn't go deep with anything!

I didn't focus on any one topic. I just threw a bunch of shit at the wall and hoped it stuck. None of it did. It wasn't because of the course! It was because I didn't drill down into any one thing. I didn't focus on one project or one site.

Instead, I mastered starting projects and not seeing them through until completion.

Looking back, there was one important takeaway though. I DID something. I was trying. I didn't spend my time wisely and I failed at everything I started, but I started something… Lots of things actually.

1.3 TRAPPED IN INACTION

Most of the time when tragedy strikes, people are trapped by inaction. They don't know what to do so they do nothing. They complain and tell everyone about their struggles.

That's the wrong thing to do. Take that time that you'd be complaining and DO something. It doesn't matter if it's the right thing or not. If it's not right, learn from it and move on.

But, if it's working, keep going deeper!

Don't let the world around you dictate what you can and can't do!

When I was a semi-truck driver at Pepsi, I remember one morning getting coffee before going out and jumping into my truck.

One of the other drivers came into the break room swearing and throwing himself around. Being that he was a 45 year old man, it made me smile.

Then, his boss walked in and asked what was wrong.

"Dude, you've got 200 cases going into X Grocery. Do you know how hard it is getting pop in there?"

His boss didn't say anything, but the driver kept laying into him…

"I work my butt off for you and I don't get an ounce of acknowledgement. You're so worried about selling cases in that you forget about your drivers…"

Finally, his boss held his hand up in the air. "Imagine how much earlier you'd be getting done today if you didn't spend the last 20 minutes throwing your temper tantrum. Just get it done."

With that, the driver stormed out of the building and he drove away.

To me though, it was an incredible realization. How much time do we spend worrying about 'woe is me' and 'why did this happen to me' when we could be actually doing something to move past whatever has us so upset.

1.4 QUICKEST PATH TO CASH

There is a very important concept that I want to share with you that has made me a lot of money long term, but I wish I would have thought of in my down year.

That concept is 'Quickest Path To Cash.' I'll reference it as QPC throughout the rest of this ebook.

When you're brainstorming your next move, write all your options down. Maybe it's starting a membership website, doing consulting, writing a book or writing a blog post…

Look at that sheet of paper.

Ask yourself, "Starting right now, which option is my Quickest Path To Cash?"

When you come up with your answer, that's what you need to do.

Back in 2009, I had a few websites that I let sit because I was looking for my big win… I was starting site after site, leaving a lot of what I built in the past sit unattended.

I was so busy looking for the big payday that I totally disregarded the gems that I had.

Looking back, if I would have been thinking about 'QPC,' I would have realized that if I started posting affiliate reviews and content that helped people solve problems, I'd start banking some pretty serious money much earlier on.

The sites are both about 4 years old and has some pretty serious Google rankings and traffic…

In 2010, I finally figured out the power of those sites… And they represent a lot of my affiliate income now.

But if I would have figured out my own QPC and would have taken action at the heart of my depression, I'd be that much farther ahead and we wouldn't have had to live in such poverty.

NOTE: Quickest Path To Cash can be anything you like. If you're looking to lose 20 pounds, it'd be more like 'Quickest Path To Thin.' If want to find the love of your life, it would be 'Quickest Path To Love.'

Just remember, whatever you want out of life, figure out what pieces of the puzzle will get you there fastest, and then act on those right away.

1.5 FIND JOY IN A SMILE

During the depths of my bout with failure, I found a couple Tony Robbins books online (http://moneysites.com/tony-robbins/). If you've never heard of Tony Robbins, he has a knack for breaking people out of their rut and on to much bigger destinies.

He isn't a motivational speaker. He isn't therapist. He does have an uncanny way of forcing your life back on track though, in both books and audio recordings.

it didn't happen...

Anyway, Tony said two things that had a profound impact in my life... He said a lot of things that impacted me, but these two I remember vividly...

The first, "Find joy in a smile."

At the time, I was like, "Dude, I'm friggin' broke. Bill collectors are calling my ass. I can't afford to eat. And you're telling me to find joy in a smile?!"

I didn't have the capacity to appreciate that statement at the time. But slowly, it started to register.

I'd see a cat lying around in the window of my neighbor's house. I'd smile to myself. Like really smile, because it was such a beautiful moment in the turmoil that is the economy and the world.

I'd think of Tony's quote...

Or I'd watch a random stranger help an elderly woman with her groceries when I was walking out with my box of pasta and sauce... And I'd smile.

Tony's quote again.

Today, I have to say that I have an incredible appreciation for so much in my life. I love my family. I love my friends. I love you for reading this book. I love all the people who come to our sites every day. I love the thousands of people who open up my emails and listen to me banter every week. I would do anything to help them win and to help them succeed.

Payment or no payment - I don't care. The more I help others, the more I feel true satisfaction with my life.

The weird thing is that my bank account has grown in direct proportion to doing good for everyone else, which is awesome.

1.6 BURN THE BOATS

The other thing Tony Robbins said in one of his videos online was:

"If you're going to take the island, you've got to burn the boats"

Don't do anything half-assed. If you're going to do it, do it right. Make it a priority. Don't allow yourself to fail.

Learn from everything!
If you try something and it doesn't work, AWESOME! Now, you know what not to do next time.

Screw up enough and you'll have a wealth of information because you'll know all of the ways it DOESN'T work and you'll be that much closer to finding something that works! Unfortunately, I had to go broke before I realized this important concept…You don't have to.

Just know that failure is the surest path to success that you'll ever find.

it didn't happen...

1.7 NO WAY OUT

If you're at a point right now that you don't think there's a way out, I assure you that there is.

If you're girlfriend just broke up with you and you want her back bad enough, you'll get her back.

If you're broke and need a way to raise some money, you will. You need to focus on it like you've never focused on anything before in your life.

If you've bought eight 'make money online' courses in a row and haven't had ANY success, you will.

In all these cases, it is possible to turn the whole situation upside down **through a very simple, very precise sequence of actions.**

Notice, I said 'actions.' Nothing, and I do mean nothing, is going to happen unless you DO something.

When I was little, I hated decisions. My mom would tell me I could choose one toy... I himmed and hawed over which one I wanted. I hated decisions because it meant that I was going to be 'without' one or the other...

As I grew up, I took a new view on decisions. I decided that as long as I chose one of them based on a solid rationale and based on my morals, I couldn't lose.

If I chose poorly, I'd learn from the experience.

If I chose wisely, I'd learn from that as well (and enjoy whatever the choice was…). Taking action is similar…

DO SOMETHING.

It doesn't matter what you do, as long as you do it.

Sometimes, this 'Ready, Fire, Aim' approach sneaks up and bites you in the ass… For example, in the first ebook I wrote and sold online, I forgot to do a few things like number the pages of the book, which really upset some people.

There were some misspellings in the text and in the Power Points… I can guarantee that there are some issues in this book as well.

But it got done!

I think I delivered an impressive course for a very, very good price. I am proud of it and I think it's one of the best local marketing courses out there… It's not perfect. It never will be. There will always be little mistakes and blunders in it.

The reason? I am much more effective if I only worry about getting 99% to perfect. By obsessing over the last 1%, the small details that truly don't matter, I won't have ANY time to devote to continuing my own education and helping others with theirs…

The bottom line is that if you take action and learn from it, you can correct mistakes in the future. You can always go back and edit but you can't ever reclaim lost time.

it didn't happen...

All it takes is a little bit… A small deviation in what you do or how you act. That small deviation is enough to alter your life drastically, for better or for worse.

What I want to show you in the following pages is how to break out of the cycle you're in, so you can reach out and grab what you're truly meant for… That might be fame or fortune or re-invigorating a relationship or paying off all your bills.

It doesn't matter.

The pieces are all the same. The process is identical.

The secret is in applying it… And DOING SOMETHING!

2

self assessment

Before you can do anything in life… Before you can achieve anything… You've got to be very clear about who you are and what you do.

Now, I'm not talking about your job… Or your role models… Or how you fill your free time. I'm talking about who you are at your core.

Think about your passions? **What brings you joy?**

Is it spending time with your kids? Or rescuing animals from the shelter? Or surprising those less fortunate for a bag of groceries on their patio the day before Christmas?

I'm not talking about all the superficial stuff like shopping or spending money or sitting down watching the biggest flat screen TV on the block…

Or even sex or drinking or drugs…

What warms your belly with good feelings? What do you experience that is strong enough to bring a smile to your face?

self assessment

I used to work at a grocery store when I was 16. Besides my Internet marketing career and helping offline businesses, it was probably the best job I've ever had.

Anyway, I was a cashier and a cart pusher. Every Sunday, when I was on register, I would have a pretty regular stream of shoppers. People I had 'checked out' in the past…

It was funny because my line was always longer than the other cashiers, but it was ok. It helped my day go by a little faster.

Among the regulars (yes, even cashiers have regulars…) were a mother and daughter. The mother was about 50 and the daughter was probably 30 or so. I never saw them without each other.

One day, the mother told me that the reason they always came through my line was because her daughter liked me. Not in the weird '30 year old likes a 16 year old' way. She thought I was pleasant and liked talking.

See, the daughter was legally blind. She always had her hand on the shopping cart and never left her mother's side.

But you know what? She was the happiest person I've ever met. Being blind, she discovered who she was at her core. She was able to find joy in the smallest things because the smallest things were what mattered to her.

To this day, if I find that I'm having a bad day, I ALWAYS look back on that moment and think, "How much do I have to be thankful for? I can see. I'm healthy. I can make my own choices and live my life the way I want to... What makes me think that I am ALLOWED to feel bad about myself and my situation? None of that affects who I truly am - so why worry about it?"

That brings me to my next question... **What do you enjoy doing?**

Playing basketball? Hanging out with friends? Learning new things? Meeting new people?

Me... I LOVE good conversations. Give me a good conversation and a cup of coffee and I'm at peace with the world.

Or pets. I love animals. Wild. Domesticated. Doesn't matter. I'll rescue every one of them when I figure out how.

I love working out. Sure, there are the obvious health benefits that go along with lifting weights but do you know why I'm addicted to it? Because it gives me time to think... To process.

At the end of the day, I enjoy knowing that I did something. This book. That course. This relationship. That email. Those are all successes in my book. I don't do anything for money anymore, even though two years ago I had none. I do things to advance my own personal development.

The funny thing?

When I started counting my days like that, I started making a lot more money because I stopped spinning my wheels and I started **doing something**!

2.1 THINK

When's the last time you thought? I mean really 'thought!'

Like you set aside time in your busy day and **stopped reacting**... My guess is it's been a long time.

Almost everyone I know (including those that I love very dearly) do nothing but react.

From one thing to the next, everything they do... Every action they take... Is based on reaction.

They react because their car broke. They react because they got a collection letter in the mail. They react because they're kid was late to pick them up.

They never sit down and THINK about anything! There isn't ever any new information processed!

When I was little, I used to always make fun of my grandpa because he'd just sit in his chair and look out the window.

He was a brilliant man, in his own right. At least that's what I remember him as being. We called him Pup-Pup but his real nickname was Skip.

Pup-pup was pretty introverted. He marched to the beat of his own drummer. He'd take all day mowing the lawn if that's what he felt like doing...

What I didn't realize back then was that his 'thinking' was what made him great. By sitting down and pondering thoughts and mental images and experiences and conversations, he was able to extrapolate an incredible amount of information because he formed the neural networks in his mind that allowed thoughts to link up together.

My friend Ron Herman often says, "There's no more new information, just old ideas uncovered." How true! The beauty of what happens online right now is that everyday people are able to easy publish their own take on old information!

It's one of the cardinal rules of bloggers... Keeping up with news is a zero-sum game. There will always be sites out there that will do it better than you.

But by putting your own twist on whatever it is you're writing about, you're able to make it your own. You're able to speak your voice and establish yourself as a credible source BECAUSE of your viewpoint!

Quite frankly, this book isn't anything new. The steps that I'm outlining are simply my take on breaking through barriers. They're things that worked for me. I'm hoping that I can present it in a clear and concise enough way that they'll help you as well!

self assessment

But it's just my take. It's the culmination of my experiences, my thoughts and a good deal of THINKING!

Personally, I need more alone time to process than others. It's a symptom of being me. You might have adequate time in the car ride from the office. Or you might need to sit down and ponder your week every Friday afternoon.

I want you to know that that's ok! You are doing yourself a disservice by constantly reacting to your environment. Tell your wife or your husband, "Honey, I need some alone time. I have some things I want to think about."

Sure, it sounds weird, but it's the only way to truly live in the moment and live life for all it's truly worth. The flipside is that if you don't set aside time to think, you live your life reacting; bouncing from one problem to another… From one situation to another… And then you're breathing your last in some hospital somewhere, wondering where that time went? Where did your life go? What did you do?

The answer… unfortunately… would be 'reacting to everything else around you.' No new ideas. No new thoughts…

Just reactions.

Living life on someone else's path.

I don't want that to be you. I want you to live a complete, full life where you find joy in everything around you and live life to the fullest as your own person - forging your own path.

2.2 GET TO KNOW YOURSELF

As you start to think and start to ask yourself very deep questions like, "Who am I at my core? What do I enjoy?" A funny thing starts happening. You start to put together a picture of who you truly are.

At first, you might not like that picture. You might very well discover that money plays a much bigger role in your life than it should. Or that 'things,' possessions, are what drives you. Or that you constantly need to compare yourself to your friends and see how you rank.

If that's you, 'CONGRATULATIONS!!' You're getting closer.

The first step in any breakthrough is being able to admit to yourself that you messed up. Or that you've got some very bad behaviors that need to be fixed. Or that there are things about yourself that you don't like.

We all feel that way. I felt that way. The person you bumped into at the coffee shop this morning feels that way. Your coworker who sits in the cubical next to you feels that way. The folks who attend church with you feel that way.

For those of you that like the picture of who you are, my guess is that you already had an idea of who you were and what you stood for. You've been actively improving your stance on life for a while now.

self assessment

Those of us who repress our true feelings about ourselves are generally the ones who think it's easier to dismiss them than deal with them.

Now, who would I be in writing this if I didn't share with you my own self image, after weeks of trying to figure it out…

Mind you, this realization came at the darkest part of my life… The part you read about above. No money. Lots of bills. No job or work. Very little going for me…

Jason Drohn's Self Assessment (2009):

The Good

- A good guy. Nice. Always smiling. Introverted. Afraid to ask for money. Semi-worried about what other people thought. Intensely devoted to family
- Loved pets. Loved animals. Enjoyed coffee. Loved technology. Believed that technology would save me. Loved conversations.
- Constant learning. Always looked for mentors through audiobooks and video sessions.
- Always optimistic. Knew that I'd 'make it' one day

The Bad

- Ashamed because I was a failure. Didn't know how I was going to pay bills. Afraid to go outside because I was afraid the cops or bill collectors would get me. Depended on my mom to feed me.

- Desperate because I couldn't figure out how to make money online. Tried to start about 38 projects hoping that one worked (none did). No focus.
- Incessantly blasting affiliate links online because I thought it was easy money.
- Starting lots of stuff but not doing any very well.
- Overweight and not doing anything about it. Depressed. Miserable. Wondering why this could happen to me. Convinced that it was Karma somehow paying me back for something.
- **Thought I deserved the shit I was being dealt.**

Overall, I was a friggin' mess.

I was ashamed, desperate, lacked focus and miserable.

Looking back, that's easy for me to say to myself. It's a little rough admitting it to you but I think it will really help you admit some of these same feelings in your own self-assessment.

Ashamed. Desperate. Those are really strong words and I don't use them carelessly. It's just how I felt.

Now…

Now that you know that it's ok to feel that way, it's time to figure out how to break through; to crush those feelings of inadequacy and regret and to start taking action…. Right Now!

self assessment

The steps that follow… Are powerful. Don't disregard one of them. If you want to break out of the lifestyle you're currently experiencing and are looking to take your life to the next level - to live with greatness - continue reading. The following strategies will get you where you want to go…

But first, we need to figure out where that is. :0)

3

goals and planning

What follows is your plan on breaking down barriers and living the life that you are truly meant to live. To experience the success that you can only dream about. To have such a high level of joy in your life that you won't want to sleep…

3.1 SET GOALS BASED ON SELF ASSESSMENT

The first thing you need to do, no matter how shitty you feel or have been feeling, is to set goals for yourself.

Find an old notebook or an empty one that your kids aren't going to be using any time soon. Take a permanent marker and title the notebook. It can be something as simple as 'Goals' but I urge you to use a word that is synonymous with 'goals.'

Very simply, the word 'goal' is almost cliché anymore. You've set goals for yourself in the past, right? Maybe you made it a goal of yours to pay off your car early. Or to lose 15 pounds by summer. Did you achieve that goal? Maybe yes. Maybe no. But it's ok, right? It's just a 'Goal.'

See what I mean? I don't like the word 'goal' because in our fast paced world, goals are easy to leave unachieved.

My goal notebook was actually titled, "Destinations."

My way of thinking is that a destination is something that you actually hit. If you're planning for a trip, you hit the destination. If you're celebrating Thanksgiving at Grandma's, your destination is her house! And you get there!

That's what I was thinking at the time, anyway.

I also included the year. So, my notebook was 'Destinations 2009.' I've since done one for 2010, 2011, 2012 and 2013.

Anyway, in this notebook, I want you to write down your goals.

Now, there is a specific process I use when I am goal planning. I set long term goals and short term goals. Often, the short term goals are considered milestones. Those milestones lead up to long term goals.

For instance, I had a lot of debt. So, in my Destinations Book, my long term goal was to 'Pay off all bad debt."

My short term goals was the individual bills themselves. Credit Cards. Student Loans. You can think of them as milestones in accomplishing the larger 'Pay off all bad debt' goal.

Other goals were to pay off my mom's house, buy an H2 for me and a new Jeep Grand Cherokee for my girlfriend, and to write two books: a business book and a fantasy book (because I love the world building of books like The Lord Of The Rings…).

Now, make sure that your goals are not monetary in nature. "I want to make $100,000" or "I will make $1 Million." They're ok goals but they're lacking because you haven't qualified it.

If you want to buy a $500,000 house, write this down instead:

"I want to move into a house with 4 bedrooms, 3 baths, a big kitchen with counter space on either side of the room, and a spacious living room with two fireplaces, of which I will pay cash."

See how you actually envision what that looks like in your mind? See how it makes you quantify that goal?

Another thing that is necessary in planning out goals is a deadline. Put it on a timeline. "I want to move into the previously stated house, by Nov 1, 2011." "Or by April 20, 2012."

Don't worry about being realistic because you will start moving in the direction you need to in order to accomplish your goals.

You will start behaving and making choices as you would if you were already in possession of the money required to buy that house.

** Disclaimer: This is critical in the process of breaking down your barrier and acheiving success! Get up from your computer or put down your ebook reader, find a notebook, and write down your 'destinations.' **

3.2 VISION

Now that you have your goals written down, I want you to read each one of them aloud. After you read each one, close your eyes and think about what that will look like.

Imagine walking through your new house. What does the entryway look like? How did you decorate it? Are there pictures on the walls? Or maybe the painting that your sister made for you for your housewarming gift? Is there a carpet covering the hardwood floor for people to take their shoes off on?

Walking into the kitchen, notice the color of the countertops. How is the sink set? Is there a window over it? Imagine where the coffee pot is and where the refrigerator is located.

Turning around, you see the living room. Imagine the giant leather sofa that you and your husband curl up on when you watch the football game. And the dogs hanging out underneath your feet as your cat perches himself on the end table, observing the activity of the house…

(I often say that our oldest cat, Magic, actually owns our house and just lets us live in it :0))

Do you see how powerful that is?

See how it is WAY more focused than, "I want to buy a $500,000 house."

I've always known that I've wanted to teach people how to do stuff. It's my passion. I love going in, learning something new, and breaking it down into the simplest of elements… Then transferring that knowledge to others.

I remember sitting on the porch, eyes closed, thinking about this future interaction I was going to have with the students of the college I graduated from.

I was going to be in front of them, presenting on what it takes to build businesses. Like, TRULY what it takes.

I'd reach into my pocket in the middle of my lecture and pull 23 $100 bills out of my pocket. One for each student in the class. And say:

> "I'm giving you each $100. You can do what you want with it. It's yours to keep. But, if you want to travel this road with me and let me teach you how to build a business… It's going to cost you exactly $100.

For that $100, you get to join my team and see what it's like to build a business from the inside out, so that you can then go out and build your own business. One free of bosses and time commitments and doing things because you have to…

If you join me, you'll be doing things that you want to and changing the world in the process."

At the time, I didn't have $2300 that I could give away. I didn't even have $2. But, I had the idea and it helped me solidify my vision. That vision of helping people travel their own path…

I want you to have similar visions of what you will do with your life. Your business. What you're passionate about. As soon as you can put yourself in that place, you'll be able to begin working toward it.

3.3 WHERE DO YOU WANT TO BE

The true power of goals is in figuring out where you want to be in a year. Or three years. Or five. And constantly working toward getting there.

You'll find though, that goals change. They take on a life of their own. As you plot out the path of where you want to be, you'll find that there are things that will pop up which alter your destination.

There is something SO powerful about focus that it is unmatched by any other force. When you find a focused person, you'll know.

They are calmer than normal people. They are quick to turn down anything the deviates from that focus. That allusiveness makes them attractive to others who are open to it.

Not to mention, when you have a very clear path laid out for yourself, you will ALWAYS be able to check yourself. Every new idea, every new thought, every new opportunity can be weighed according to your path.

It's like having a personal mission statement (which we'll go over in the next section). You can weigh everything according to that mission statement. Is it something I agree with? Will it get me to where I'm going? Will it detract from my desired outcome?

These are all internal dialogues that you will begin to have once you pick your destination…

3.4 REDEFINE SUCCESS

The first thing that I always do when I have a goal planning session is to 'redefine success.' It's a very simple mind-tweak that I learned from my good friend Travis Sago.

When he first taught me, it was in relation to a course I was putting together and how to structure the follow-up sequence. (Like I said, this book is no holds barred…)

Since he taught it to me, I've become aware that everything I've been able to accomplish is because of this simple, little tweak and I am becoming more and more suspecting that that's why so many of the great people in history have been bankrupt, poor and lost… Because they didn't understand that big successes are simply a result of small successes.

When you're broke, either of mind or spirit, even the smallest, most trivial success is monumental.

It might be that your favorite brand of coffee is on sale, and something you can finally afford. Or that an awesome training course has a 30-day $1 trial that you can use to scoop up all the information and cancel before you get billed again. Or having a Facebook conversation with someone you've liked for a long time…

Those things are monumental! They're insignificant in most people's eyes. Most people take it with a grain of salt. But, for those who are down on their luck and trying desperately to regain their footing on life, they make all the difference in the world.

Why do you think so many kids squander their inheritance? Or so many lottery winners spend endlessly until they are right back at their previous position in life? It's because they don't know success. They aren't intimately familiar with hardship…

When you're rich, you don't think that way. You think that success is making a few million a year. Or having the most gorgeous spouse in the world. Or driving the fanciest, most expensive cars.

Frankly, none of that stuff matters. If you can't find success in starting a forum thread that takes off like wildfire, or in an email that's sent thanking you for your work, then you won't ever know what big successes SHOULD feel like.

Now, in redefining success, the strategy is pretty simple. Take what you think success is, and chunk it down into the smallest of actions.

(The next chapter is going to be all about actions and how to break down your actions into doable steps, that, when completed, are small successes… I merely want to introduce this line of thinking here so you can see it in the light I'm trying to portray.)

If you want to move into a $500,000 house, there are small actions you can take that are achievable.

In achieving them, you get your first taste of success.

For instance:

1. Go online and find the general area that you want to live in.
2. Take rides in that area so you can see what the neighborhood is like.
3. Compare prices of homes in that area and take special note of what they're selling for.

4. Call a realtor and have a conversation about the area…

Each of those actions, when completed will give you small successes that build on each other.

Like I said, in the next chapter I'm going to teach you about taking action, but just know that the result of taking action is having small successes :0)

3.5 PLANNING

The final stage in goal setting is planning.

My dad had a favorite saying, "If you fail to plan, you plan to fail."

Again, those words fell on deaf ears when I was 6, but I can't tell you how much I appreciate them now!

If you take a macro look at your goals, you will find that they probably follow a pattern. For instance, mine were things like:

- Pay off my bills
- Buy 2 new cars
- Get a bigger house so we could start a family…

I quantified them, of course, but that was the gist of it.

What I did was draw a little flowchart connecting up my goals.

So, before I bought 2 new cars, I'd have to pay off my bills. And I wanted to replace our old Jeep with 2 cars BEFORE I bought a new house (because the house we live in is fine for what we need it for now...

So, that would look like this:

It was important for me to plan them out this way because then it gave me focus on accomplishing one goal, then another, then another...

I was focused.

I wasn't running around, calling a realtor and getting excited about a new house way BEFORE I paid off my bills.

I was able to put a clear perspective on what I needed to be doing and when.

goals and planning

Now, there are probably some things that can and should happen at the same time. That's ok. It might look something like this:

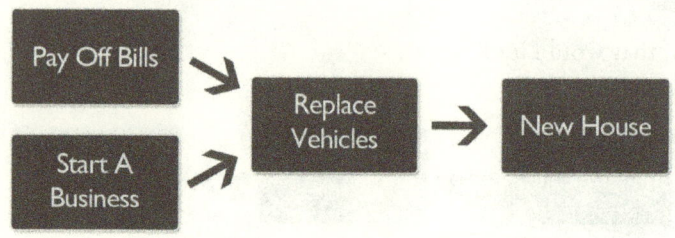

And that's ok! It should be as easy or as complex as you think it should be. It's going to change over time as new things get added or things get taken away... The important thing is that it's done! You will always be able to refer back to it, compare yourself to it, and tweak it as you see fit.

AND CONGRATS!

Congrats on your first success. I literally mean that. Take a minute and think about what you've just done and how it's going to shape your life.

Let it sink in.

You've just done when 99% of the people in the world wish they could!

You've DONE something. You now have a plan of action. You've got a map that you can forever tweak and compare your actions to.

Phoenix Formula

I am seriously sitting here writing this and ecstatic for you because you have just taken the biggest step in breaking through your barrier… Of realizing the life you want.

4

taking action

I've got to admit, this chapter is going to be the hardest for you. Taking action.

It's so easy to sit by idly and wish that you could have success. Or that you could own a business that basically prints money. Watching other people take their turn at the speedbag…

So many people are trapped by inaction. They want to make sure they have all the information… Or they're waiting for the 'right time.' Or they're 'so busy.'

Believe me. I know.

I read a really good article once that talked about taking action. I forget who wrote it, but I found it online, talking about how being perfect isn't a reality…

The writer was explaining how it's easy to continually put something off because it's too difficult or because of not having enough time.

He then went into a rant about nothing is ever perfect…

taking action

You'll never have 100% of the information you need to get started. You'll never know 100% of the process. Most of the time it's simply because things change. You're going to have to adapt as it goes. That's part of life. Adapting.

It's easy to start something and get 80% or 90% of the way there. YOU WILL NEVER ACHIEVE 100%! It's a fact of life. Things change so fast.

Imagine if I didn't put out our training products on building profitable websites at MoneySites.com because I needed to think about it more or because it wasn't edited by a professional.

Imagine if this book wasn't ever published because it wasn't perfect.

I know it won't ever be perfect! There are ideas that it contains that could use more fleshing out. There are bound to be misspellings. The pages might not be numbered. The logo might look a little blurry. The format of the copy could be a little bit more on-point.

But, all that stuff would mean that I would delay the release, hopelessly trying to perfect something that could change a lot of people's lives!

Think about Apple. Their iPods were released and there were bugs. The technology wasn't as good or as well thought out back then as it is now. But they launched them anyway.

They committed to always making them better and better, hence the revisions and the newer, faster models...

Some of it is that Apple wants more of their customer's money. Some of it is that they constantly want to increase the quality of their product. If they didn't launch because they were waiting for the 'perfect mp3 device,' they wouldn't be anywhere close to the revenue targets that they're hitting now!

They wouldn't have singlehandedly built the market for mp3 devices. They wouldn't have had their incredible success with iPhones or iPads.

They'd still be selling desktops, laptops and software...

Taking action and doing something is NEVER perfect. It can't be. It's impossible. But taking action and tweaking results is absolutely possible. It's how fortunes are made. It's how success happens. Most of all though, it's how we, as humans, grow.

4.1 PERSONAL MISSION STATEMENT

So, the first thing we need to work on is your personal mission statement. Your personal mission statement is very much like a corporate mission statement in the fact that it should help you focus all your energy on 'doing something.' It should also help you measure up everything else to whether or not it's a good direction for you to be moving in or not.

taking action

Here's what I mean.

My personal mission statement is along the lines of helping people and businesses succeed and surrounding myself with people smarter than me…

If I am invited to an event filled with the top minds in Internet marketing or business, I should look at that invitation more closely because it aligns with my personal mission statement.

If I am asked to co-write a book on seduction and dating, I'd turn it down because it doesn't look at all like my personal mission statement. (not to mention, I know nothing about that particular topic…)

You see how that works?

Life is actually far easier when you have a statement like that prepared because it takes all of your decision-making out of the equation. It either aligns or it doesn't. Bottom line.

It's a bit like on Sesame Street. Remember the game, 'Which of these is not like the other?' If something doesn't fit, you just don't do it! Or you take it out!

It's that easy.

Here are some suggestions in creating a mission statement which I learned from Stephen Covey. (from Stephen Covery's site: https://www.stephencovey.com/mission-statements.php):

- Write down your roles as you now see them. Are you satisfied with the mirror image of your life?
- Start a collection of notes, quotes, and ideas you may want to use as resource material in writing your personal mission statement.
- Identify a project you will be facing in the near future and apply the principle of mental creation.
- Write down the results you desire and what steps will lead you to those results.

Stephen Covey is where I first heard of the idea of personal mission statements. The idea is to write a quality statement that defines:

- Who you are
- What your roles are
- What you want to accomplish
- Where you want to be

That statement can be 20 words or 200, it doesn't matter. The only requirement is that it uniquely fits you.

Now, I've changed mine in the 2 years since I originally wrote it because of new outlooks and experiences. I think that's ok. It's a part of growing and evolving. Just keep it memorized so that you can constantly check yourself against it.

4.2 ACTION LISTS

You've come a long way! You know you have. I just wanted to take a minute and pat you on the back for it.

This journey isn't easy. It requires some serious self-examination and the results can be scary. So scary, in fact, that most people avoid it like the plague. They would rather just keep living their lives, forever ignorant to what's going on inside them.

Now, is where you start to see success in its most quintessential form.

This is a difficult section. I want you to know that it's also the most important to breaking free. What I'm about to tell you has literally made people millions upon millions of dollars. It's led to the world's greatest inventions and the greatest achievements in our time…

And, I have never seen it spelled out.

Why that is, I don't know. The way I see it, it's the most crucial component of anyone looking to advance in ANYTHING. It's the biggest reason people fail. And it's the root of every success known to man…

It's taking action.

Not just any action though… Small, micro-actions that lead to bigger achievements.

With each of those micro-actions, comes with it a mini-success as it's achieved.

That's why I introduced the idea of redefining success earlier… So that you could let that stir in your mind a little bit before we got here.

The basis of action is as small and as trivial is a to-do list… Or it can be as large as a project. In either case, the action requires steps that need to be performed in sequence.

What I want to teach you is how to build that sequence of steps.

Now, just so we're clear, you might not totally understand what is involved in breaking one of your goals down into micro-actions. That's ok. Let's figure that out first.

One of my goals is to open up a non-profit.

I've just added it to my 'Destinations' notebook.

That non-profit, I'm thinking, is going to be related to pets, namely dogs and cats. I have an innate need to save every living thing on the planet. I've got 4 dogs, all of which being either rescued or adopted.

That's my thing. My dogs are like my kids, seeing as how I don't have any of those yet.

taking action

Now, mind you, I have no idea how to start a non-profit. Frankly, I don't even know what non-profits do.

Think about it. We know of the Red Cross and Walks and other charity organizations… But do we know what they do with the money? Or how they collect the money? Or how they raise the money? Or what the structure of the company looks like?

You might, but I don't!

So, in approaching the idea of starting a non-profit, I consider that I'm going to need some time to do research so I'm a little less clueless.

… I can research online.

… I'm sure there are books and stuff out there that will help clarify my thinking.

… I consult with a couple non-profits so I can get a meeting with their CEOs

… I know a non-profit development manager (marketer). I can take her out to lunch and see what I can find out.

After those steps, I can then look at actually forming the non-profit itself. Here are some things that I'll need to do:

- File a 501c3 (that much I do know…)

- Figure out who's going to be on the Board of Directors
- Figure out what the non-profit is going to do (aka. Who it's going to help…)
- See what I need to do in terms of getting some initial funding
- Get logos and a website made
- See about getting some press coverage in my local area

Those (I think) would be the first action steps in actually starting a non-profit. BUT, those could change depending on costs involved and what my research yields.

The idea is to break the big thing, starting a non-profit, down into manageable tasks.

Can I email the Development Director of one of the non-profits I help and offer to take her to lunch? Yep. If she accepts, I get to pick her brain. That's a mini-success! Hooray!!!

Is it possible that that conversation will determine the action steps in forming the non-profit? Absolutely! Perhaps she knows something I don't.

Do you see how any big project can be broken down into smaller actions?

The same can be done for buying a house. Or writing an ebook or a book. Or patching up a relationship. Or traveling to China.

They are all, simply, the sum of their micro-actions!
Alright, now that I've sufficiently confused you, let's nail down and **Action List.**

These are actions that I will need to take to form my non-profit.

(Notice that they are quantifiable, as in time, location, and conversation medium.)

Non-Profit Action List

- Stage 1: Research
  1. Spend 1 hour researching how to set up a non-profit online, from authority sites
  2. Post a message on Facebook and Linkedin asking if anyone has good resources that I can learn more from.
  3. Look for ebooks on Amazon/Kindle/iPad about starting a non-profit
  4. Call Hugh and see if he's got any non-profits in the animal world that he can introduce me to on Tuesday.
  5. Email Melissa and see if she can join me for lunch so I can ask her questions about what it takes to market a non-profit and raise money. Specifically ask about events and fundraisers. Ask her for contacts in event management and catering.
  6. Call John and see if I can schedule some time to talk about what is needed, from a legal standpoint, to start and operate a non-profit.

- Stage 2: Setup
  1. File a 501c3 with Adam (lawyer)
  2. Ask John, Melissa and Hugh to the board of directors. Ask them if they know of anyone else who's a good fit.
  3. Get in touch with 3 local shelters or organizations and ask them what they need in terms of equipment, supplies, or money.
  4. Schedule first fundraising event, at the end of March, with Melissa's help, paid or unpaid, where I can raise awareness. Get media involved.
  5. Schedule 6 hours to design a logo and get a site up for the time being. It will be perfected before rollout by a third party organization.

- Stage 3: Rollout
  1. ...
  2. ...
  3. ...

Can you see how crystal clear that action list is? It is literally begging to be checked off. The thinking is all done. All that's left is simply performing those actions.

If I have a team or an assistant, I can meet with them and figure out what they can do and what I need to do. If I'm doing it myself, I just schedule time and go down the list!

Oh... And thank you for humoring me. I truly have no idea how to start a non-profit, but this is the action list I'll be using to get one started :0)

I wanted you to see the thought process and what was needed to create one, for real… Not something conjured up for sake of example.

This process can be applied to anything! Believe me. It might be something like getting your child to respect you. Or getting your ex boyfriend back. Each involve action steps.

If it's your ex, the first couple actions might be writing a letter to them. Then, a phone call. Or perhaps going out and having fun with your friends!

Getting your child to respect you might be: taking them to a movie, establishing new common ground, doing something they like to do, helping them with cleaning their room…

Now, what's next is scheduling it.

You can have to most killer Action List in the world, but if you don't physically schedule a time where you promise yourself you'll do it, it won't get done.

4.3 SCHEDULE TO ACT

Now, you've got your goals and your action list. You're doing an awesome job. Has anyone told you that yet?

The last part, before you start achieving your goals, is to schedule them!

Now, I don't mean schedule your goals... I mean schedule the actions that will deliver your goals to you!

Going back to the non-profit action list, I need to set aside time in my schedule to take that action list and DO some of the tasks.

So, what I do, is open up Google Calendar (http://google.com/calendar).

I see that next Thursday I have an opening in the morning, at 9AM. Now, knowing that I prefer to work on stuff like this in the morning, I schedule it.

I give myself two hours to implement Actions #1, #2, #3, #4. Those are:

> Spend 1 hour researching how to set up a non-profit online, from authority sites
1. Post a message on Facebook and Linkedin asking if anyone has good resources that I can learn more from.
2. Look for ebooks on Amazon/Kindle/iPad about starting a non-profit
3. Call Hugh and see if he's got any non-profits in the animal world that he can introduce me to on Tuesday.

In looking at the action list, I see that I have 2 additional actions that need to be performed, so I schedule them too.

taking action

The following Monday, I have 11AM open, so I block off an hour. In the note section of Google

Calendar, I write the following:

- Email Melissa and see if she can join me for lunch so I can ask her questions about what it takes to market a non-profit and raise money. Specifically ask about events and fundraisers. Ask her for contacts in event management and catering.
- Call John and see if I can schedule some time to talk about what is needed, from a legal standpoint, to start and operate a non-profit.

After a little while, my calendar will sync up with my phone, so I won't have any choice but to perform the action list!

Now, all that's left is keeping to my calendar!

You still aren't out of the woods yet.

YOU NEED TO READ THE NEXT SECTION – RIGHT NOW!

4.4 THE EPIC DOWNFALL?

WARNING: Alright. You're good up until this point… You've planned your goals. You've broken them down into action steps… BUT you might still fail.

Let's say you scheduled your action list next Wednesday. Everything is moving along just fine. Wednesday morning rolls around. You get off the phone with your mom, who's complaining about her property taxes. Your kid just hit you up for $30 to go to the school dance…

Your phone goes off. You pick it up and there's a little readout that says, "Action List: Set Up A Non-Profit."

What do you do? Worry about the chaos going on around you? Or follow through with your word and actually sit down for two hours and DO check off your actions?

This is where most people fall off the wagon. They have brilliant ideas and ambitions. They have well thought out action lists. Their buzzer goes off to start DOING something and they don't.

They're too busy. They don't have enough time. They've have to go put out this fire or call that person…

None of that stuff gets you closer to your goals.

You might as well throw this book out (or send it to the digital labrynth of death known as the recycle bin…)
Don't give it a second thought.

Your goals?

Not attainable.
Your dreams?

taking action

Forever out of reach.

Why?

Because you have decided that taking care of temporary problems, like throwing another load of laundry in the washer or trying to find that form you had to fill out for your son was more important than the goal that you want to achieve…

Forgive me. I'm being hard with you. But I want it to serve its point.

It's SOOOOO easy to push off something as small as an action list.

After all, these are just little actions… They won't serve any major function, right?

Completely. Utterly. Totally. Wrong!

These little actions are the basis of your goals and dreams. They should be revered. By doing them, you are placing yourself on the pathway to success, fortune, and esteem…

Whatever it is you want.

It starts with an action.

Don't put it off.

Not for one minute. Not for one second.

The most important thing you do in your life is on that little action list because it will define you. It will grow. One thing leads to another, and another, and before you know it you are making decisions from a completely different station in life…

All based on a stupid, little action list.

Powerful?

You bet.

I want you to succeed. I really do. In whatever you want in life. For you to come this far in this book is a tremendous accomplishment and I'd hate to see you back down now…

Take what's yours. Know that you deserve the best the world has to offer.

It's as simple as that.

Take action.

4.5 TO DO LISTS

Sometimes, actions are larger than they appear at first.

For instance, in my non-profit action list, in the second stage, one of them is to get a logo and website done.

taking action

For me, that is a pretty singular action because it's something I do often.

Most people would need to break that down into smaller steps though. Or they might need to designate elements of that action to different people or team members.

Let's look at that a little deeper.

The action is 'Logo and Website Design.'

That might look something like this:

- Pick the colors of the logo
- Have 5 logos designed and choose one of them
- Find websites that I'd like the non-profit one to look like
- Choose website colors
- Choose website layout
- Get quotes from web designer
- Choose a quote
- Set up initial meeting
- Pay web designer down payment
- Set up follow up meetings
- Do final tweaking
- Give final payment

See how easy it is to just simply check those off now?

Also, see how the to-do list makes the 'generally complex' process of getting a website design done relatively easy!

Now, all that's left in order to complete that action is simply to work through the to do list!

The beauty of to do lists is that you can actually work through multiple actions at the same time if you're sending work to a third party or if you have staff that's doing it.

If you're doing it yourself, you can batch tasks so that you're making two or three calls in sequence, rather than doing them individually.

I know that for me, it's easier to get my mind in one place, such as writing, answering emails or making phone calls, and have it stay there for longer periods of time.

If I start moving between doing one thing and then another, typing and talking and answering questions, I get terribly bogged down and I don't get much accomplished at all.

For instance, when I am building a training course or writing a book, I:

- Start with a mindmap (MindMeister is good for this: http://mindmeister.com)
- Move to doing up all the powerpoints and 'content.'
- Take two or three days and do nothing but record
- Then save them in raw format.
- Do all editing
- Encode them all
- Upload them all

Don't worry if that's a foreign language to you. I promise it won't be on the test!

Batching stuff helps me get it done quickly and efficiently. It also lets me submerge myself in a topic and not come out until it's done. That's where I get my best ideas and do my best work – when I've been working on something for a few hours.

This book for example, is a product of my submerging.

I don't write this thing unless I have at least 3 or 4 hours of uninterrupted time, which usually means the weekends.

Why? Because it is forcing me to focus… I can't be as deep as I am, with the thoughts running around in my head, and answering questions about Internet marketing or picking up clients…

I wouldn't be able to communicate on a level nearly as compelling as this.

4.6 WHAT'S WORKING?

After you start implementing your action lists (and your to-do lists), I want you to ask yourself a very simple, self-examining question.

"What's working now?"

For those of you who are looking for money, what is making you money? Right now?

For those looking to get their ex-boyfriend back. What is working on him? What are you doing that's getting his attention?

If you're trying to correct your disrespectful teenager, what's working? Have you done something that's temporarily snapped him out of his funk?

In any case, think about the answer…

Oftentimes, we look for a magic bullet. Something that fixes the problem immediately…

In most cases, that magic bullet doesn't exist.

Change is a process. One that you MUST be patient with.

The change from being broke to not having to worry about your bills will take time. Your ex-boyfriend? He'll take time to come back. There is a process there that must be dealt with.

The joy though, oftentimes comes in that process! In those mini-successes. One smile. One sale. One sign-up. One telephone call. Those are all things that can be expanded on.

We, as humans, tend to be a little idiotic at times. When something starts working, we, for some reason, think that it's not working fast enough or good enough or whatever, and go out searching for a new solution.

Perhaps the only issue is that you haven't done enough of what's working!

Honestly!

I want to tell you a little story.

Back when I first started out online, I had a blog. I was enchanted by this thing called an 'ebook' and how people would pay like $20 for it and download it to their computer.

Well, I wrote one, did a little bit of sales copy, and put a buy now button on it.

Now, when most people do that, they think that they'll be instantly filthy rich, but I was smarter than that. I knew that traffic would be slow going, so I started a Google Adwords campaign (http://www.google.com/adwords/).

The ebook was about how to buy and sell domain names, otherwise known as 'Domaining.' It was a good, entry level book about how to find ideas for domain names, how to buy them, how to sell them, how to 'park' them, etc.

Anyway, I set up an Adwords campaign targeting all the hot button keywords like "domaining, domaining ebook, buy and sell domains, etc."

I set up a campaign to start at $10 a day. For that, I could get about 30 clicks back then... And wouldn't you know it! I sold a few. In fact, I was spending about $250 a month on advertising and I was making about $600...

For the math majors in the room, that's a profit of $350...

Now, keep in mind, this was about 5 years ago. Well before the digital product boom and the 'make money online' era. And LONG before the push button millions!

Looking at this little, measly ebook, making $350 a month with a little bit of advertising expense, you'd think, "Geez, just increase your ad budget and keep testing!"

After all, if I had a client in the same position, that's what I'd tell him!

If I could give you $1 and you gave me $2 back, I'd be a complete moron if I didn't completely clean out my bank accounts and give you every penny I had...

Well, you know what I did?

I sold the site!

I figured I hadn't touched in in a while and I wasn't comfortable spending any more than $10 a day on advertising so I sold it!!!

A completely viable business. A tested and working product. One that spun off cash WAY before the big Internet product/ebook boom…

And I sold it.

(Can you tell I'm still beating myself up over it?!)

Now, if I would've examined the site and the revenue, I would have seen that EVERYTHING was working. The sales copy. The traffic source. The ebook. It was all there!

I would have ramped up traffic to the moon and collected money from the backside of it.

… But I sold it.

Oftentimes, the things that are working in your life are already there, you're just not conscious of them. And the only way to actually become aware is to temporarily set aside your grief, your turmoil, your struggling and ask, "What's working right now?"

"What's going right in my life?"

It doesn't matter how much heartbreak or distress you're in, there IS something that is going right.

… It might be a conversation with a friend.

… It might be handing the boy outside Walmart, who's collecting money for cancer research, your last dollar.

… It might be that good feeling that you have being overly friendly with the cashier at Dollar General.

Concentrate on what that feels like. What does the smile feel like? What goes on in your mind as you freely give away your last dollar?

Let those thoughts seep into your consciousness…

Eventually, those memories and those thoughts are going to be the fuel of your success.

It won't be about making $1,000 in a day. Or finally getting your ex back. Or successfully starting your own business.

It WILL be about the journey. The people you've met. The things that you've taken pleasure in. The gifts that you've given.

It's the strangest thing in the world, but I promise you it works.

The task is easy.

Concentrate on what works and do more of it.

Period.

4.7 ONE PATH

There is something we refer to in the Internet marketing industry called 'shiny-object syndrome.'

If you have it, don't worry. I am hoping to break you out of it in the next 1000 words or so.

Shiny-Object Syndrome is very simply, the need to acquire any new device, course, or gadget that promises to offer value.

For some people, it's Apple's products. For others, it's Internet marketing courses. Still others, it's a different date partner every night.

Sometimes it's a phase. Sometimes it's a way of life.

The problem about chasing shiny objects is you're forever bouncing between any number of things.

There is no focus.

Remember in the last section when we talked about 'batching'? The reason batching works is because it forces focus. It forces you to maintain sustained energy on one task, a similar set of tasks, or on one thought.

If I were trying to write this book, bouncing between emails and stats programs and jumping on and off the phone, what would the quality of this document be?

Moot, right? (I think that's a word :0))

Now, another example. Hundreds of thousands of people a year try to make money online. Do you know how many succeed?
Less than 2% make money at all.

Less than .04% make more than a couple hundred dollars a month.

Far less than that are able to quit their jobs for their marketing career.

Why is that? Is it that the market is saturated? Nope. Are the newbies doing it correctly? Usually. So, what's wrong?

Focus.

The people who sell Internet marketing products and 'make money online' products have gotten into a cycle where they release a new product every month or so that promises to deliver a push button system for affiliate riches.

The newbies buy it.

They implement it for a few weeks and nothing happens…

Right about that time, there's a new product launched that is similar to what they already bought, but different enough to bring in new customers. They buy it. They fail.

Another product introduced…
You get the point.

What happens is the newbie goes in, has either no or lackluster success, buys a bunch of stuff, and exits the market telling all their buddies that 'it doesn't work.'

It's not that affiliate marketing doesn't work. Or that the Clickbank vendors are selling crap (although sometimes they are)…

It's that the newbies didn't give any of the models enough time to mature!

Shiny object syndrome, I believe, is why most people fail at a lot of things. Relationships. School. Money.

One way to combat that is to figure out what's working and do more of it!

If you're having success, why change anything?! It's something I've never understood, even though I've done more than my fair share of the shiny-object thing…

Simply ramp it up! Scale it! Do more of it! Hire people to do it for you!

Focus!

4.8 DON'T GIVE UP

Don't ever give up. No matter how bad things in your life are, don't give up. Do what you need to do to pay the bills, but don't ever feel defeated! You're better than that. You've dared to dream and believe that you're better than your current station…

And you are! Don't let anyone tell you otherwise.

One of the reasons I put so much importance on 'doing more of what's working' is because it forces you to focus on the good things that are going on around you.

If you're mind is clouded with all the things that are happening in your life, you won't ever be able to see the positives that are going on all around you.

Worse yet, by focusing on the negative, you might lose your will to succeed altogether – resorting to something other than you innermost goals and ideals.

Look at Thomas Edison:

> Thomas Edison was interviewed by a young reporter who boldly asked Mr. Edison if he felt like a failure and if he thought he should just give up by now.
>
> Perplexed, Edison replied, "Young man, why would I feel like a failure? And why would I ever give up? I now know definitively over 9,000 ways that an electric light

bulb will not work. Success is almost in my grasp." And shortly after that, and over 10,000 attempts, Edison invented the light bulb.

Granted, we aren't inventing anything nearly as grand and world-changing as the light build (well, you might be!) but our goals and our dreams are ours to keep and accomplish.

I have heard more multi-millionaires and uber-successful people say that they were inches away from giving up, only to decide that they were going to stick it out…

Their loans were coming due. Their businesses were falling apart. Their customers started drying up. But they decided, after a long and grueling process, to stick it out. For better or worse.

Shortly after, their true successes started piling up!

Success is never sudden. From the public perspective, when we hear of a new hip-hop star and she's all over the news in the blink of an eye, it's not that she was put there instantly! It's probably that:

A. She has a hip-hop father who owns a record label
B. She has worked her way up, building mini-success on mini-success until it hit critical mass and then there was worldwide adoption

The beauty is in the process. We all love to hear about people's life and their background. We enjoy hearing about how some celebrity grew up on the streets, had a terrible home life, and made it to be an icon in our own culture.

Those stories are uplifting because we can ALL relate to them in some way or another. The villain is the streets or poverty or a broken home. The hero is the actor's willpower to increase their quality of life and endure despair, desperation and face immeasurable odds…

Only to win the day and have the fame and glory bestowed upon him at the end…

It's the classic tale, repeated over and over in theaters and cinemas all over the world.

Think about those tales. The lead character:

- Never gave up even though he should have
- Stood for his beliefs no matter what
- Looked adversity in the face and said, "Do your worst!" (taken from the movie, *The Count of Monte Cristo* – I love that movie.)
- Defied all odds and adversity

And we as a culture love those stories! We'll love yours too… Just don't ever give up so that you can tell us :0)

4.9 INSPIRATION

When you feel like you have nothing, you will find inspiration in the weirdest of places.

For instance, the movie I just talked about, The Count Of Monte Cristo, I loved this passage:

> Life is a storm, my young friend. You will bask in the sunlight one moment, be shattered on the rocks the next. What makes you a man is what you do when that storm comes. You must look into that storm and shout as you did in Rome. Do your worst, for I will do mine! Then the fates will know you as we know you: as Albert Mondego, the man!

I had watched that movie a million times but never pulled that passage out or let it affect me like it did when I was broken.

Another thing I do is re-read books. I have a collection of books that have served as my favorites. Every few years, I try to crack them open again and go through them.

The reason is simple. Every reading offers new understanding.

The things that I passed over two years ago without so much as a thought now come alive with meaning because I have new experiences or new thoughts.

The things that I thought were important a few years ago, are almost inconsequential now!

It's really pretty crazy…
The reading is changed by what is currently held in your mind.

The first time I read *Think and Grow Rich* by Napoleon Hill, I picked out line after line about being broke and how to get past it.
I just reread it a few months ago and I couldn't even find the passages that so affected me. Rather, new ones lit up my mind and had a drastically different meaning.

It's magical.

One thing I would highly recommend is opening up an Evernote account (http://evernote.com) or grabbing an old notebook and tearing out all the used pages. Keep it as your inspiration notebook where you collect passages and thoughts that affect you positively.

They might be pictures if you're a visual person. It might be quotes or sayings. It doesn't matter, as long as you find it uplifting.

Words have a strange way of transporting you to an alternate plane of existence… Somewhere far away from your current location where the world is perfect and anything is possible.

Let your inspiration notebook reflect that.

In building on that, let's talk for a minute about a mundane task, but something that I really want you to do… Journaling.

4.10 JOURNALING

If you're a guy reading this book, call it your journal. It's somehow more manly. If you're a lady, this would be your diary. :0)
This task is simple, and it may be combined with your inspiration notebook. I wouldn't advise that though.

Your inspiration book should be something you can open up and almost instantly feel better. It should provide semi-immediate gratification, no matter how bad your day is going.

Your journal… Is to collect your day's activities and thoughts.

Because we are interested in 'actions that will break you out of your rut,' I tend to think of my journal more in a way of recording actions. The four questions I ask myself are:

1. What did I do?
2. What am I doing?
3. What will I be doing?
4. What are my bottlenecks?

What these questions force you to do is to DO SOMETHING and report what you've done. It's almost as if you're in school, being graded on your performance. If you do something, you get an A. If you don't, you fail.

In it's most primitive form, these questions are going to evoke a general response that you can write in your journal. But… They force you to check yourself against what you've done.

It's definitely ok to add to the content of the journal entry. Maybe you want to write about how you felt or what your emotions were those days... Or how people reacted... Or talk about your first success... Or the joint venture partner you ran into...

It doesn't matter what you write, as long as you write something! Everyday!

4.11 STOP BUYING STUFF

This is something that I feel pretty strongly about, but people might get a little disturbed... Stop buying stuff! No more information products. No more gadgets. No new movies or games. Stop spending money.

First of all, if you're broke, you shouldn't be buying this stuff anyway. By definition, if you're broke then you don't have any money. I know there are things like credit and all those other 'buy now, pay later' devices, but you're just digging your hole deeper.

Secondly, by continually adding things to your life, you are adding to your distraction. You wouldn't believe how GOOD it feels to totally clean out your closet, removing all but your top 7 outfits... Not combinations of outfits... 7 tops and 7 bottoms. With 2 pairs of shoes. That's it.

No distraction. No clutter.

taking action

No spent mental energy.

All that's left - pure focus…

Now, your situation might not be rooted in money. That doesn't matter though. I really think that a lot of spending is done to serve as a distraction to life in general. Shopping to some people makes them happy.

It helps ease their mind. It helps them deal with the reality of their life. At what cost though? More junk? More clothes? Something else to think about? Something else to pay for?

Remember, back at the beginning of the book when we talked about self-examination? This is where that comes in! Being true to yourself and those around you…

I really want you to be intimately aware of what you're doing and why you're doing it. Is it a reaction?

Is it a need?

Are you thinking for yourself?

You should be. Don't let marketers make choices for you… (Coming from a person who LOVES marketing!) Don't endlessly chase the newest, hottest thing. Get things straight in your life, focus on the needs, and then you can cater to your wants.

4.12 EATING RIGHT

Wait a minute! This isn't a diet book…

Well, it could be I guess?! The rules of Phoenix Formula can be applied to dieting just as well as business or relationships or parenting…

This is actually going to be a quick section though. It's something that I just recently discovered…

Eating right is not only a good practice in terms of body weight and overall health, but can also aid in mental activity…

As you can imagine, certain nutrients and vitamins are crucial to healthy brain functions… That's not what I'm talking about.

What I'm talking about is the correlation of overeating to laziness and lack of work and focus!

Back in my dark days, we couldn't afford anything more than spaghetti and sauce. That's not an overly healthy dinner. If you're reading this and want to eat healthier, write it down on your action list as something you can work towards…

Recently though, Chelsey and I started doing a lot of super healthy dinners, supplemented by multivitamins, protein shakes and meal replacement bars.

taking action

At first, I just wanted to try it and see what my productivity looked like. It also helped that I wanted to lose about 40 pounds!

I found that if I had lunch my brain shut down... So I decided to start:

- Drinking a protein shake in the morning for breakfast
- Eating a meal replacement bar at 10:30AM or 11AM
- Eating another meal replacement bar between 2PM – 3PM
- Eating a healthy dinner at 5PM – 6PM
- (possible) smart snack at 9PM

What I've found is that by keeping these meals to about 200-400 calories, I'm able to keep a pretty high brain function throughout the day. It doesn't matter if it's 8AM or 4PM, I'm good to tackle anything. Before, I was ready to get out of the office at 2PM and I was terribly inefficient overall after lunch!

I eat something every 3 hours or so, all the way up until about 8 PM. The later meals are more heavy in protein so that excess carbs don't convert to fat when I'm sleeping.

I take one cheat day a week, which is usually Saturday. So, if you're planning on taking me out to dinner, Saturday is a good day to do it!!

The other side of this 'smaller meals every 3 hours' is that it keeps your insulin levels pretty constant. Now, I'm not a doctor or a nutritionist by any means, but I find that I have a nice, steady supply of energy day in and day out. As opposed to eating two or three big meals where my insulin levels spiked and then died off.

So basically, small meals every three hours. Pay attention to your energy, productivity and focus. And watch excess pounds fall off. It's like magic, really!

4.13 EXERCISE

Now, to the other side of diet and fitness? Exercise.

I've been lifting a long time. When I was younger, I was pretty heavy into powerlifting. At 17, I could bench 470 lbs. which was pretty awesome.

Well, as I got older, that muscle started to shift :0) And it forced me back into the gym for some maintenance.

Now, there are lots of books on the market that will show you how to work out and exercise. This isn't one of them.

I will highly encourage you to do some sort of activity that you enjoy doing… Not only because it's good for you and it'll help you remain physically fit, but it will also give you alone time that you can use to clear your head.

You'll find that you'll have your best ideas and brainstorming sessions when you're actually up moving around.

taking action

It might be a quick morning walk. Or driving to the gym to work out. Or playing catch with your dogs… Something away from the hustle and bustle, outside…

Movement spurs innovation. It also helps you feel better about yourself and (coupled with dieting) will shed pounds pretty quick. Both of which will improve your self-esteem and your own personal productivity.

Now, when you envision yourself delivering the keynote at your industry conference, you'll be able to picture yourself 30 lbs lighter! That's a pretty good feeling, huh

5

surroundings

The last chapter was focused heavily on internal feelings, actions and reflection. Now, all that stuff is good, but it isn't everything you need to know.

There is a very powerful influence in your life that you have no control over... That's what we're going to talk about in this chapter.

That influence is your surroundings. The people you hang out with. The media that you consume. The external pressures that are forced upon you.

Take a minute and think about the last 24 hours. How many times have you heard that someone was broke? Or that someone lost their job?

How many times did you witness neglect or road rage or someone giving another person an excuse?

Those are all negative influences that you shouldn't have to put up with.

I want you to treat your mind like a vault. Be very cautious about what you let in. I'm not saying close yourself off to the world, but be very aware of what's going on around you, how it's making you feel, and what it's causing you to think.

In the coming pages, I am going to teach you how to filter what's coming into your mind and act and live the way you want to live, regardless of your position in life.

The fact of the matter is, if you act like who you WANT to be and do the things that the person you WANT to be do, you'll end up being the person you WANT TO BE… I've got to thank Travis Sago for that piece of wisdom!

5.1 NO MORE NEGATIVE

Back in 2009, during my dark days period, I was pretty caught up in the media. See, I've never been very political but I found myself watching a lot of CNN and Fox News during the first Obama election.

As you know, that was about the same time that our economy was collapsing. The stock market was at a severe low and everywhere you looked you heard stories of layoffs and businesses closing their doors.

All that negative news fueled me, and not in a good way.

What happened was that I started to feed into the media. I started using the economy as my excuse. "Businesses all over the country are failing because of poor economic conditions, it only makes sense that mine is failing too…"

In reality, the economy was just an excuse.

If you take a closer look, there were many businesses that thrived! Most of them were headed up by good management or had solid, innovational principles at work.

One day, I got fed up with it. I told myself that I wasn't going to let anything else enter my mind that was negative.

I stopped watching the news. I stopped talking to people who were negative. I didn't read the paper. I focused ONLY on accomplishing my goals.

If the media I was consuming wasn't solely devoted to relaxation or achieving my destinations, I changed the channel.

What followed was a profound shift in perspective.

The farther I got away from negative influences, the more mini-successes I had. Those mini-successes started building up into major successes.

I started thinking more positively about the economy and the times we were living in. I started feeling better about myself.

As I write this, I can honestly say that I don't ever watch the news. I try my best to stay away from any negative influences, whether that be friends, acquaintences, anything I read or television programming. I try not to give excuses…

I can say that the absence of negative media has affected me so dramatically that when I hear other people's conversations, I pick up the negative vibes and language almost immediately. Whereas, before I might agree with it or take part in the conversation… Now, I just dismiss it.

When you take all the negativity out of your life, you start to recognize your surroundings. You start to listen to your and engage in conversations.

If there is anything with a negative connotation or if you find yourself giving excuses, stop. Dismiss them from your mind. Don't agree with the person you are speaking to simply to agree and keep the conversation moving forward. Ask them what they mean by what they just said. Try to figure out the reason that they're stuck in the negative mindset. Notice how it's affecting their life and what they have going on around them.

Do your best to avoid negativity in all apsects. Think purely of the positive and you will start living that way.

5.2 FRIENDS

I am very careful about the friends I keep close to anymore. As I said in the previous chapter, I stay away from negativity, but that doesn't necessarily qualify the kinds of friends you want to keep.

Ever since I shifted my mindset from negativity and feeling limited, I started attracting a different caliber of friends to me.

All of a sudden, within a couple months, I started talking to people who were more successful than me, living for goals and dreams.

Think about the friendships you have now. What are their purpose?

Every friendship has a purpose. Sometimes it's to complain about work. Sometimes it's because of ulterior motives like dating or sex. Sometimes it's to go shopping or go to the Friday night football game.

Think about whom you have around you. Why are you friends with them? Do you TRULY enjoy their company? Is it someone you can just hang out with? Or do you have to be doing something?

I think it's important to quantify friendships because each one was built because of something. If that 'something' is negative, end it. The friends you keep are more influential in your life than you know.

If you friend is endlessly complaining about how everything is SO expensive at the store, and he's always broke, and he barely has enough to pay his bills, it's time to figure out how to get out of that relationship.

Why? Because by you listening to all this, you'll start to use that same excuse in your life… When you should be spending your time trying to come up with a solution!

The longer you sit and listen to him, the more brainwashed you will become. I promise you.

5.3 FAMILY

While we're on this negativity kick, I want to throw in an exceptionally challenging one.

Family.

I am very close to my family. We are all pretty tight. My brothers and my mom and I talk a few times a week. That's just how we are.

Luckily, my family is pretty positive for the most part. We are good influences on each other. I have helped a number of people break out who have had very negative family situations though.

So, what do you do when your family is a source of negativity? You can't just stop talking to them. You can't ignore them. So what then?

The answer is to coach them.

You're going to have to sit them down and tell them, point blank, that you don't want any more negativity in your life. You want them to do their best to NOT COMPLAIN, NOT TALK BAD ABOUT SOMEONE ELSE, AND NOT TALK ABOUT HOW BROKE THEY ARE.

That isn't a small feat.

Here's the deal though, they are going to ask you why. "Why are you being like this?"

That's a perfect time for you to teach them about your new success experiments. If you can help them adopt the same strategies that I lay out in this book, they are going to be able to improve the quality of their life as well!

It's a win/win situation but it will be hard at first. I know it will. It's got to get done though.

If you're best friend and biggest source of negativity and stress is your mother, you're going to have to handle it.

5.4 MINDSET

You've heard me talk a little about limiting mindset and I want to explain that to you. There are too major mindsets – a limiting mindset and an abundance mindset.

There are countless books written about mindsets and although important, I think action is more paramount to success.

I really feel that people get trapped in the 'abundance mindset' mentality because it's easy. Then, when nothing happens, they start wondering about the validity of the concept. The missing ingredient is action.

That's what this ebook is all about. Taking action. Without action, no goals or dreams are ever accomplished, no matter how 'abundant' you think your life should be.

So now, let's talk about limiting mindset.

Limited Mindset

Limiting mindset is where you tell yourself that something is not possible. Then, usually, you follow that up with an excuse.

For example, I could have said,

"There's no way I'm going to make $100 a day in affiliate income. I don't have a good email list."

"I won't ever be able to buy that new car, I only make $400 a week."

"We're never going to be able to go on a trip like that, I'll never be able to afford it."

In fact, you don't even need an excuse!

"I can't buy that house…"

"We won't ever be able to go skydiving…"

"They will never like me. They're too successful…"

"I'm never going to get to go to Disney World…"

Do you see how all those statements are limiting your conscious and subconscious mind? They are telling you that you can't do something.

As soon as you pick up the distinction, you are going to hear those statements all around you. Your boss. Your family. Your friends. Everywhere.

Someone is ALWAYS going to be saying that they can't do something or that they can't buy something or that they can't go somewhere… It's simply not true.

You can do whatever you want!

Abundance Mentality

The opposite of a limiting mindset is abundance mentality.

As I mentioned earlier, people use the abundance mentality as a crutch. They think that if they adopt this mentality and see themselves in possession of $1 Million dollars, they will be, almost overnight.

What they forget about is action.

Action, or more notably 'taking action', is the fuel that makes the abundance mentality work.

Now, when thinking abundantly, no goal is too high. No success is unachievable. No obstacle is too hard to overcome.

Whether you picked it up or not, honing and training your abundance mentality was what we did in the 'setting goals' section.

I intentionally masked the notion because I wanted you to step through the process I used in breaking out of my cycle.

Back then, the idea of doing something as grand as starting a non-profit or going to conferences or paying cash for a house was just simple TOO BIG.

But, I knew that if I set my goals to something I could achieve, and broke those goals down into micro-actions and to-do's, I'd have an easier time achieving them.

What I want you to know is that nothing is impossible as long as you set goals and take action.

Life has this funny way of presenting to you what you need to accomplish your goals AS LONG AS YOU ARE TAKING ACTION. It's a bit uncanny.

I have seen it on both sides of the coin, when I needed someone or something, and when other people have needed something from me.

Usually, through a weird series of events, the solution presents itself.

For instance, one of my goals was to get out in the community and start attending more marketing and business events.

I stuck my neck out and went to my first on in 2010, and met some of my best friends. Then, shortly after that, the world basically pulled me into another event, where I met some more people who helped me with my first product launch...

Another instance, where I was needed, was for my now friend, Allana Pratt. She had all these web elements put together. A few ebooks. Spots on television and radio. She just needed the drive and an idea that she could 'hang her hat on.'

After meeting her and a few phone calls, we came up with an idea for a teleseminar series that she's running with. I'm excited because I was able to help her connect the dots and coach her through the business/make money aspects of it and I know that she's going to have a lot of success because of that coaching.

surroundings

The world has a mystical way of presenting you with the path as long as you are actively doing something to accomplish your goals.

Things will start to happen to you precisely when they're supposed to. An introduction here. A realization there. An opportunity here. All of it adds up.

In order for the world to know what you want, you have to make it known. You've got to open up your mouth and put yourself out there. You've got to meet people and talk about your goals and your ambitions.

If you are too afraid to talk about that stuff, or present that stuff in any way, you need to figure out how to take micro-steps in that direction. Maybe it's a Facebook status update. Or an email to a friend. The medium doesn't matter. You have to be willing to put yourself out there just a little bit and see what happens.

You can't just sit in your room and dream that one day your life will be different. You've got to go out and do something about it!

5.5 NEGATIVE ATTITUDE

Ever since I was little, my dad always taught me that having a positive attitude was paramount to success.

In fact, he gave me this drawing and I hung it up on my door when I was about 10 years old:

It's funny because the irony of this image is that I was days, maybe seconds, away from giving up totally and I just couldn't bring myself to it.

I couldn't throw in the towel.

I knew that I would be able to accomplish great things. I knew that I would be able to make a difference in people's lives. I knew that I had enough knowledge and experience to make people a lot of money in business…

I just didn't have the correct mindset to see it forward.

My dad always made me examine situations and bring the positive out of them. Back then, a loss in a basketball game would be tough, but he'd make me see that I had an 89% free throw percentage, or that I got 12 rebounds.

He'd make me see that failure in a different light.

Today, I know that I went through 2009 so that I could truly appreciate what was coming. I would be able to appreciate wealth and friends and a successful business. I'd be able to give back to the community and concentrate less on money and money-getting and more on delivering value and results.

I also know that no matter what happens, I am able to shine a positive light on it. There are two sides to every coin. One is usually more apparent than the other.

5.6 BE AROUND PEOPLE THAT ARE BETTER THAN YOU

Everyday, I make a conscious effort to be around and to talk to people that are smarter or better than me in some way.

Mike Hill has a great video on his blog about 'Are you networking up or networking down?' (http://mikehillsblog.com)

That's a bit too business'y for this application, but think about it. Are you constantly surrounding yourself with people who are smarter than you? More connected than you? More successful than you? More compassionate than you? More experienced than you?

If not, you should be.

What happens is that when you are around people who challenge you, spiritually, emotionally or intellectually, you start acting and behaving that way. You start to think about things like them. You start to understand their point of view.

More importantly, you start to expand your own thinking.

One of my favorite things to do is talk and become friends with people in completely different verticals and professions.

For instance, I have friends who are certified therapists, police officers, paramedics, fire fighters, doctors, real estate agents and CEO's of for-profit and non-profit companies.

Some of them are clients. Some are people that I'd call to go out to lunch. At the end of the day though, they are all my friends.

These people are very, very good at what they do. They force me to think in terms of their business, which helps me expand mine.

I, in turn, force them into thinking about what I do and they start to adopt some of those principles.

surroundings

In either case, the varied knowledge and experiences forces me to grow in ways that aren't determined. It forces me to think of new things and make new connections in my mind… Connections that very few other people possess.

To me, that's one of the most fascinating things about life and friendship. Connecting with people can send your world spinning in a much different, much better direction.

One thing I do want to point out though is that you should always be checking your personal mission statement against the 'direction' that your life is going. If it's something that serves you, let it ride. If not, dismiss it.

That's the beauty of the personal mission statement. It can always serve as a point of balance in your life where you can refer back to what you want.

5.7 SHOP AT THE STORES YOU FEEL GOOD AT

I hope this doesn't sound trivial, but this was a big proponent in breaking out of my downtrodden cycle.

As you've read in this chapter, it's important to be around people who believe in you and who are better or smarter than you in some way.

I also think that you are who you associate with, on a general level. Where you shop. Where you go and get your hair cut, or where you go eat dinner.

Phoenix Formula

There is an area in my city that is more affluent than where I currently live. I think that there are sections like that in every city…

In this 'more affluent section' there is a grocery store named Wegmans that Chelsey and I really like. When we were broke, we couldn't shop there because it is a bit more expensive than Walmart or some of the ones closer. Not to mention, it's about 20 minutes away and we couldn't really afford the gas to get there.

Well, little by little, we would get some cash freed up and we'd do our weekly shopping at this nicer grocery store. It was a treat. A micro-success.

Then, as times got better and better, we started making it a weekly habit to do the bulk of our grocery shopping there.

Now, Wegmans is a little bit more expensive, but the atmosphere is amazing. If you've never heard of it, they've been in the 'Top 100 best places to work for' for something like 8 years. This year, they were #5 (http://money.cnn.com/magazines/fortune/best-companies/).

At Wegmans, people go shopping and graze the produce. They say excuse me if they pull their cart out in front of you. They say please and thank you to the clerks. The Wegmans employees are exceptional. They're always pleasant and they seem truly happy to help you with your grocery buying experience.

I'm a bit partial to Wegmans actually because it was my first job, when I was 16. I pushed carts and did some cash register stuff. To this day, it's still my favorite job (as in working for someone else…).

The reason we shop there is because we feel good about it. We like the pleasantness of the people who are shopping and working. We enjoy the atmosphere. The place is filled with people in nicer clothes who shop with their families…

Not to mention, where it's located is where we'd like to live someday. Nothing super rich or super fancy, but an area where you can leave your doors unlocked and not fear for your safety. Where everyone else works and has goals and is living toward achieving something…

I strongly encourage you to find somewhere that you feel good about being. It might be a store. It might be a coffee shop. Learn to appreciate it. Reward yourself with the experience when you can and revel in it when you can do it more often.

That's micro-success in its truest form.

5.8 GIVING

There is something funny that happens when you give away your last few bucks to a worthwhile cause. No matter how broke you are, you feel good about yourself.

Anthony Robbins talks about this in one of his CD's. When you donate to charity or to help kids fight cancer, your mind automatically takes you to a place of abundance. You feel like no matter how bad off you are, you are still able to help someone else in their time of need.

Chelsey and I are animal lovers, as you already know.

With all of the abandoned animals and people who are forced to move from homes to apartments, shelters have seen an influx of animals.

So we called the animal shelter that we got our puppies from and asked what they needed, money or supplies.

Their answer was supplies. They needed bleach, laundry detergent and some other stuff.

So we went to the store and bought about $30 worth of supplies and ran them down to the shelter.

Now, $30 isn't much – but it's all we had at the time.

Every month, we did the same thing. It made us feel good because we were helping a cause that really needed it.

What happened though was that we started seeing a shift in our mindset. We started having more success and were able to give more. We started giving to people standing outside of Wal-Mart. We started donating more at the checkout of the grocery store. Not for tax benefits or anything else, but because we were being blessed with success and wanted to give where we could.

Don't underestimate giving to worthwhile causes. Notice how it makes you feel. Notice what kind of difference it makes in your life.

6

education

Education is the last and most important continuing success element in the Phoenix Formula. I am an avid believer in continuing on your path and gaining knowledge, which you then put into action.

I also believe that the best use of your increasing revenue is to reinvest in knowledge.

You already know how to put a plan to action. What's left is expanding that plan, and formulating new plans to achieve more and more success.

Your mind is a beautiful thing. Use it. Feed it. Don't ever let it go to waste. Ideas and goals and thoughts and emotions are all powerful things. Continue to learn and you will continue to grow.

education

6.1 REINVEST

One of the reasons I love home-study courses, ebooks and video training courses is that I can learn from some of the greatest minds in the world, without having to leave the house.

I think that way about books as well.

Imagine, having 5 or 6 hours of time devoted to you, by someone like Anthony Robbins or Dr. Robert Cialdini or Steven Covey or Dr. William Cohen.

I love knowledge. I love the idea that I can get to know someone by the words that they are writing and the thoughts that are going through their head.

Oftentimes, when reading, I put as much if not more mental energy into what the author is thinking as I do in reading what's on the page.

Books represent the transferring of knowledge and experience from one person to another. Bookstores are truly magical places, in my eyes.

If you're interested in a subject, make a note to research it. Write it down on your to-do list. Put a selection of books in your Amazon Wish List. Even if you don't have money now, write those titles down and buy one or two books as you get some cash freed up.

If digital courses or video is more to your liking, find some people who are doing audio and video and follow them. Save for them. Take notes as you listen to them or read them.

There are some things that I personally like to do:

- Write notes in http://evernote.com
- Write notes on paper and scan them into my computer
- Put little post-its on the pages I want to especially reference
- Break out the highlighter and mark passages that I like

After going through a course or a book, write down a little action plan on what steps you are going to implement.

It doesn't need to be anything big. Just take action on something!

6.2 THINKING ROOM

This might be a bit abstract for your needs, but I want you to think about it for a bit.

I like to sit in one chair in my office for the sole purpose of thinking. Ideally, one would have a separate room altogether for thinking… I'm not at that point yet.

The point of the thinking room is to, well, think! Devoid of all distraction. Where it's just you and a tablet. Nothing on the walls. No beeping or buzzing of a computer. Nothing. Just you and your thoughts.

Now, this might sound horrifying to some people. To others, it might sound peaceful. Really, it's just a place that you can use to download all of the information that you've taken in so that you can organize it in your brain.

It's important to do this activity at least once a week. Life catches us up and we're so often in a place where all we do is react. The thinking room helps us act, plan and put our action lists in to motion.

Think of it as quiet time that your brain needs to formulate its next move. I've found that it's crucial to success and allows you to envision your path and where your life is going. Some of my best ideas have been formulated during this quiet time!

6.3 MENTAL FUEL

The bottom line with reinvesting in education, gaining knowledge and meeting new and interesting people is that it increases your mental fuel.

Your brain forms new pathways that it uses. You start to see commonalities between not so common thoughts. You start to bridge gaps in thinking, not because of the singular piece of gaining new knowledge, but because of the new knowledge in combination with things you already know, or experiences you've already had.

I love learning because it gives me fuel for new ideas and thoughts. It doesn't matter what genre it is. It could be about psychology, home repair, remodeling, technology, and programming… All that stuff gives me a better idea of marketing or business building in general. It helps me be more effective for my clients and for myself.

Now, the dark side of having all that mental fuel is that you'll start to be scatterbrained). That's where we return to our goals and our personal mission statement and check to make sure our thoughts and our actions are consistent to what we said we wanted to accomplish.

If they are, roll with them. If not, dismiss them or write them down in a 'to be completed later' list!

6.4 PRACTICE YOUR CRAFT

The last thing I want to leave you with is the encouragement to practice your craft. Do what you are passionate about.

Passion is one of those things that radiates from our bodies and ignites those around us.

Think about brilliant motivational speakers like Les Brown and Greg Reed. Is it that their words are truly motivational? Or that what they are saying really strikes a chord with us?

Sometimes.

education

More times than not, though; it's because of their passion.

Put someone on stage who is an expert in a profession we care nothing about. Let them do their thing. If they are passionate and showcasing that passion, chances are, we'll get excited about what it is that they're saying!

The bottom line is DO what makes you happy. Do it to the best of your ability. Don't let ANYONE stand in your way of doing the thing that you love.

Then, and only then, you will find that you are truly reaching the goals and the dreams that you set out for.

Practice your craft. Take action. Adapt. Grow.

That's what life is about.

People will see you and watch you and want to be associated with you because you are someone who they want to get to know!!

7

closing

I want to take a minute and thank you for reading this book.

It means a lot to me and in finishing it, you now have all the tools you need to break out of your cycle. Believe in yourself. Believe that any thought that you have is possible.

Break your goals and your dreams down into action plans and to-do lists. Achieve mini-successes.

Never stop learning.

Get in front of people who are better and smarter than you.

Give to those less fortunate (and no matter how bad it seems, there are people less fortunate…)

Do what makes you happy.

Live your life the way you want to live it. You deserve the best!

Your friend,

Jason Drohn

www.ingramcontent.com/pod-product-compliance
Lightning Source LLC
Chambersburg PA
CBHW031406040426
42444CB00005B/434